"A hurry of hoofs in a village street...
The fate of a nation was riding that night;
And the spark struck out by that steed, in his flight,
Kindled the land into flame with its heat."

Henry Wadsworth Longfellow

My name is Samuel Adams, and I was there when Paul Revere, William Dawes, and Samuel Prescott triggered an alarm that spread across the countryside on the night of April 18, 1775.

The rights of American colonists were being slowly chipped away by King George III across the ocean. But never despair! That is a motto for you and for me. Where there is a spark of patriotic fire, we will rekindle it. In the struggle for liberty, it does not take a majority to prevail...but rather an irate, tireless minority, keen on setting brushfires of freedom in the minds of men.

Those brushfires had been ignited, and they could not be stopped. That was my firm belief as I watched the three horses, carrying three patriots, gallop into the gloom.

To begin, let me back up the story just a bit — to earlier in the day on April 18. The British troops were on the move, but so were our spies.

A source, very close to the top of British military leadership, passed a vital message to Dr. Joseph Warren.

THE LOGICAL PERSON TO CARRY THIS INFORMATION WOULD BE PAUL REVERE.

MAKES SENSE. REVERE'S WORD IS RESPECTED EVERYWHERE.

AND HE'S KNOWN EVERYWHERE. HE'S HEAD OF HIS MILITIA UNIT, AND HE'S IN SEVERAL TAVERN CLUBS AND FOUR WHIG* CLUBS.

FIVE WHIG CLUBS ACTUALLY.

One year earlier, Paul Revere carried the Suffolk Resolves to the First Continental Congress — a declaration protesting British tyranny. Now, he had a new mission.

PAUL, THE BRITISH ARE HEADING TO LEXINGTON TO ARREST SAMUEL ADAMS AND JOHN HANCOCK. THE MILITARY SUPPLIES IN CONCORD ARE ALSO UNDER THREAT.

EARLIER TODAY, A STABLE BOY TOLD ME THAT HE HEARD THE REGULARS* WERE SET TO MARCH!

I WANT YOU AND WILLIAM DAWES TO CARRY A WARNING TO ADAMS AND HANCOCK.

*American Whigs supported independence from British rule during the revolution.

*"Regulars" are British troops.

2

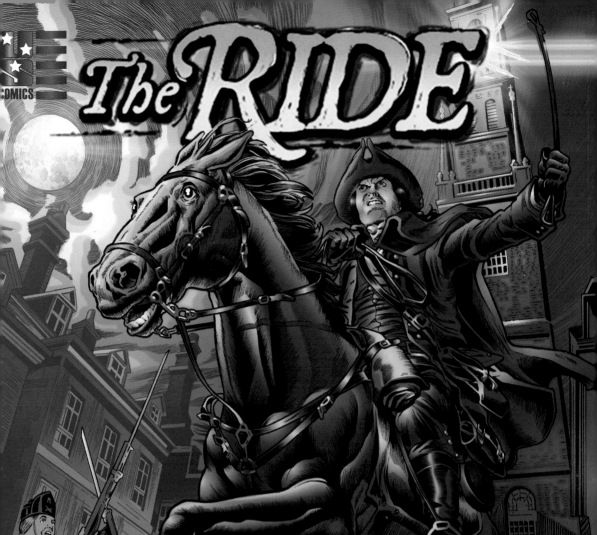

Samuel Adams
Founding Father from
Massachusetts

Dr. Samuel Prescott
Physician who carried a
warning to Concord

John Hancock
Massachusetts merchant and
statesman

Dorothy "Dolly" Quincy
John Hancock's fiancée

William Dawes
Rider who carried a warning
with Revere

Paul Revere
Silversmith, engraver, and
express rider

Dr. Joseph Warren
Physician and Boston patriot

Jonas Clarke
Minister in Lexington

Colonel James Barrett
Militia officer at Concord

Writer: **Doug Peterson**
Editor: **Kelly Ayris**
Pencils: **Joe Bennett**
Inks: **Belardino Brabo**
Colors: **Mark McNabb**
Letters: **Lisa McMahon**
Production Design: **Lisa McMahon**

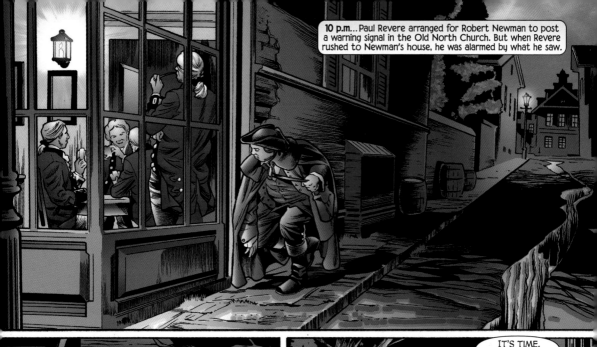

10 p.m... Paul Revere arranged for Robert Newman to post a warning signal in the Old North Church. But when Revere rushed to Newman's house, he was alarmed by what he saw.

PAUL...

IT'S TIME. DO YOU HAVE THE LANTERNS?

WE DO.

HANG TWO LANTERNS IN THE STEEPLE. BE SURE THEY'RE FACING CHARLESTOWN.

WHY ARE THERE BRITISH SOLDIERS IN YOUR HOUSE, ROBERT?

MY MOTHER IS BOARDING THEM. I HAD TO SNEAK OUT THE SECOND-FLOOR WINDOW.

THE RED DOG

While Revere headed for the river, Newman and the other two men hurried to the Old North Church.

THOMAS, KEEP GUARD WHILE ROBERT AND I TAKE THE LANTERNS TO THE TOP OF THE STEEPLE.

3

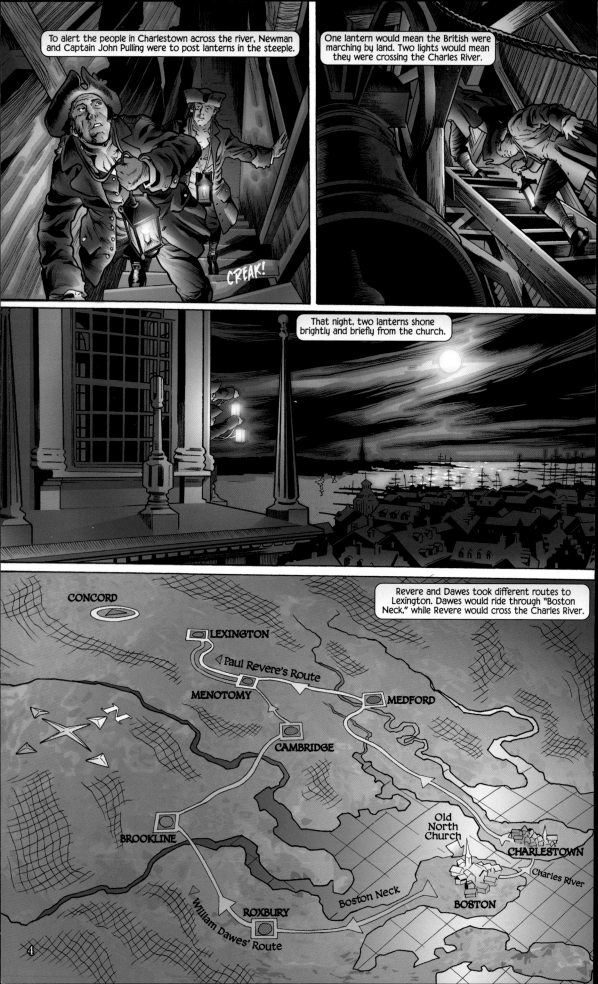

QUIET NOW.

Miraculously, Revere made it past a British warship, the *HMS Somerset*, unnoticed.

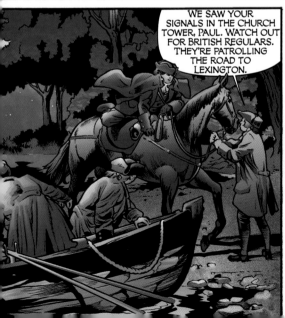

WE SAW YOUR SIGNALS IN THE CHURCH TOWER, PAUL. WATCH OUT FOR BRITISH REGULARS. THEY'RE PATROLLING THE ROAD TO LEXINGTON.

11 p.m....

CLIPPITY-CLOPPP!

Meanwhile, it took the British two hours to organize and cross the Charles River.

On the other side of the river, the march began – through swampy land.

Once the British soldiers reached firm ground, they had to wait for rations from the navy to arrive.

I'M FREEZING IN THESE WET CLOTHES.

DO YOU HAVE YOUR 36 ROUNDS?

I DO, SIR.

After waiting miserably for an hour, the food finally arrived.

DISGUSTING! BISCUITS CRAWLING WITH MAGGOTS.

YOU MEAN WE WAITED ALL THAT TIME FOR NAVY FOOD LIKE THIS?

WE ALREADY HAD OUR ARMY RATIONS ~ WITHOUT THE MAGGOTS!

Meanwhile, John Hancock and I were staying in Lexington at the home of Reverend Jonas Clarke, his wife, Lucy, and their many children. We were completely unaware that the British were heading our way.

But we knew war was imminent. Over the past several years, we had felt the boot of British tyranny.

There was the Boston Massacre in 1770!

We were heavily taxed without any voice in Parliament!

The Coercive Acts took governing power away from the people and closed Boston Harbor! Intolerable! Now, things were coming to a head.

Revere and Dawes went with us to a tavern on the Common, where we encountered volunteers from the Lexington militia.

WE BELIEVE THE BRITISH ARE HEADING TO CONCORD TO DESTROY OUR MUNITIONS.

THAT MAKES SENSE. I DON'T THINK THE BRITISH WOULD SEND SO MANY TROOPS THIS WAY JUST TO ARREST JOHN AND ME.

EXCELLENT FISH THIS.

PAUL AND WILLIAM, IT LOOKS LIKE YOUR WORK IS NOT DONE FOR THE NIGHT.

April 19, about 1 a.m... Revere and Dawes left for Concord carrying their warning. They were joined by Dr. Samuel Prescott, who was leaving Lexington after seeing his fiancée.

I'M GOING HOME TO CONCORD, SO I'LL HELP YOU DELIVER THE WARNING.

THANK YOU. WE NEED TO WARN ALL OF THE HOUSES BETWEEN HERE AND CONCORD.

By this time, the alert from Revere, Dawes, and Prescott was being carried all across the countryside by multiple riders.

THUMP! THUMP! THUMP!

CLIPPITY-CLOPP!

Militias sprang into action in Lexington...

...and in other towns – Framingham, Dover, Dedham, Roxbury, and more.

13

About a half mile from Lexington...

BLAM!
POW!
POW!

WHAT IS THAT? WHAT'S HAPPENING, REVERE?

IT'S PROBABLY A SIGNAL TO ALARM THE COUNTRYSIDE. YOU REDCOATS ARE IN SERIOUS TROUBLE.

WE BETTER RIDE BACK TO THE LINES TO WARN THE COMMANDER.

BUT WHAT ABOUT OUR PRISONER?

I'M AFRAID WE HAVE NO CHOICE. TO TRAVEL FASTER, WE'LL NEED TO LET HIM LOOSE.

3 a.m.... Then just like that, Paul Revere was freed. But he never again saw his mount, Brown Beauty.

Revere spotted the lights of the Clarke parsonage.

14

15

16

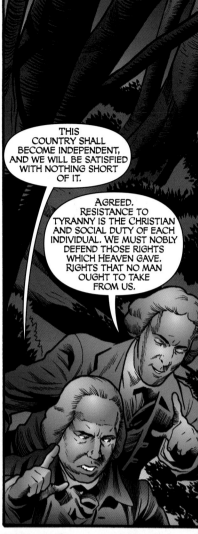

JONATHAN!

PAPA!

Jonathan Harrington died only feet away from his home near the Common.

STAY WITH US, JONATHAN!

PAPA, DON'T DIE, DON'T DIE!

British Colonel Francis Smith finally brought his troops under control. In the end, eight militiamen were killed and nine badly wounded. Only one British soldier was wounded. None died.

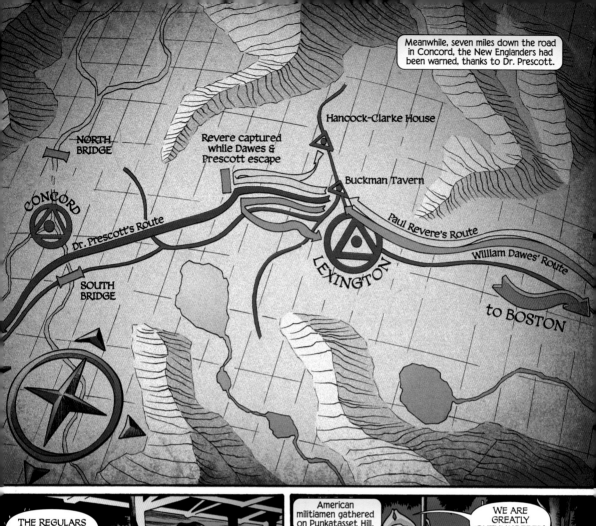

I must admit that British General Thomas Gage's troops showed some restraint in Concord. They searched for our supplies, but there was little looting...

...except someone stole a Bible and a copy of *Liberty of the Will*. Maybe the thief will learn something from both books.

Most of our military supplies had already been taken out of Concord – or cleverly hidden.

Colonel James Barrett's sons plowed their fields and "planted" weapons in the ground.

LET'S PRAY FOR A GOOD CROP OF AMMUNITION THIS SEASON.

The British found very little, other than three 24-pounder cannons buried in a yard.

The British set fire to the gun carriages and other items...

But the blaze spread!

WE MUST STOP THE FLAMES FROM REACHING ANY OTHER HOMES!

WILL WE LET THEM BURN THE TOWN DOWN?

NO! NO!

WE WILL CLEAR THE BRIDGE OF REDCOATS.

25

The militia began to march toward the British at the North Bridge.

DO NOT FIRE UNTIL THE REGULARS FIRE FIRST!

DO NOT FIRE UNTIL I GIVE THE COMMAND!

BLAM!

I DIDN'T GIVE THE ORDER!

BLAM!

BLAM!

BLAMM!

BWEEE!

WING?

CRACK!

BAM!
BAM!

UGH.....

At noon, the weary British began to march back to Boston, almost twenty miles away.

As the British retreated, hundreds of American colonials ambushed them along the road. The British fought past the ambush...

BLAM!

PING!

KRAK!

BLAM!

...only to encounter more ferocious fighters at the Bloody Angle. One British general said his troops had to retreat under non-stop fire, which was like a moving circle, surrounding them wherever they went.

POW

The British retreated to Boston – a shocking victory for the American militia.

THE AMERICANS DID NOT FIGHT US LIKE A REGULAR ARMY. THEY FOUGHT BEHIND TREES AND STONE WALLS, AND OUT OF THE WOODS AND HOUSES.

SAVAGES!

King George III was furious!

WHEN ONCE THESE REBELS HAVE FELT A SMART BLOW, THEY WILL SUBMIT!

News of the battle and the American victory spread like a whirlwind.

TO ARMS! TO ARMS! THE WAR HAS BEGUN!

28

BREEE!

POW

BLAMM

AHHHH!

HAVE YOU EVER HEARD OF IRREGULAR TROOPS, HURRIED TOGETHER AT A MOMENT'S NOTICE, ATTACKING AND DRIVING AWAY VETERAN SOLDIERS?

NEVER.

To keep the news from spreading, the British arrested two Boston newspapermen, John Gill and Peter Edes.

But Edes escaped and went back to work, printing the *Boston Gazette*. Other newspapers also added their voices.

BLOODY BUTCHER
BRITISH TROOPS
RUNAWAY FLIGHT OF THE REGULAR

Being the PARTICULARS of the VICTORIOUS BATTLE fought near CON from Boston, is the Province of the MassachusettsLorem ipsum dolor sit amet, consectet diam nonummy nibh euismod tincidunt ut laoreet dolore magna aliquam erat volut minim veniam, quis nostrud exerci tation ullamcorper suscipit lobortis nisl ut consequat. Duis autem vel eum iriure dolor in hend dolore eu feugiat nulla

29

But what happened to John and me? One month later, in May of 1775, we were greeted like heroes in Philadelphia when we came there for the Second Continental Congress. Frankly, it was embarrassing.

SMILE, SAM! YOU LOOK LIKE YOU'RE ABOUT TO BE SICK.

I JUST MIGHT BE.

The battles in Lexington and Concord will be famed in the history of America. But this was only the very beginning of the war. The fire had just been lit.

The affairs of our country were at this moment in the most critical situation. Every wheel now seemed to be in motion. But I was so fully satisfied in the justice of our cause that I could confidently, as well as devoutly, pray for our victory.

What else could I do but pray? After all, mortals cannot command success.

What triggered the war, which began at Lexington and Concord?

Tensions had been building for years, especially when the British imposed taxes on the colonies, even though Americans had no representation in Parliament. When colonists heaved 342 chests of tea into Boston harbor to protest the tax on tea, King George III decided to punish Boston severely.

The king signed a series of regulations called the Coercive Acts. Later, they would be named the Intolerable Acts. The British closed the port of Boston, throwing thousands of people out of their jobs immediately.

As if that wasn't enough, another Coercive Act took power from the people, giving the king and Parliament the authority to govern Massachusetts directly. Juries could only be appointed by unelected sheriffs, and town meetings in Massachusetts became illegal without the governor's approval. Officials were also allowed to use whatever means possible to stifle riots or impose taxes.

The punishment was severe, but many British leaders thought the American colonists would give in without a fight.

They were wrong.

"These are the times that try men's souls. The summer soldier and the sunshine patriot will, in this crisis, shrink from the service of his country; but he that stands it now, deserves the love and thanks of man and woman. Tyranny, like hell, is not easily conquered; yet we have this consolation with us, that the harder the conflict, the more glorious the triumph."
(Thomas Paine)

Who gave Dr. Joseph Warren the secret message, revealing the British plans to attack Lexington and Concord?

Dr. Joseph Warren had "special access to a confidential informer, someone well connected at the uppermost levels of the British command," says David Hackett Fischer in his book *Paul Revere's Ride*. "The identity of this person was a secret so closely guarded that it was known to Warren alone, and he carried it faithfully to his grave."

However, Fischer adds, "evidence strongly suggests" that the spy was none other than Margaret Kemble Gage, the American-born wife of British General Thomas Gage.

"The God who gave us life gave us liberty at the same time."
(Thomas Jefferson)

"Those who would give up essential liberty to purchase a little temporary safety deserve neither liberty nor safety."
(Benjamin Franklin)

Was Paul Revere a spy?

Yes, Paul Revere is credited with founding the first American intelligence network, known as "the mechanics."

Revere was born in Boston to a French father and a mother of English descent. As Fischer says in *Paul Revere's Ride*, Revere was taught that every man had two callings – a specific calling to work in a vocation and a general calling to do the work of Christ. The two callings were as important as two oars. If you tried to row with only one oar, you would go in circles.

Revere's vocation was as a silversmith in Boston, creating beautiful items – medals, pins, buckles, and teapots.

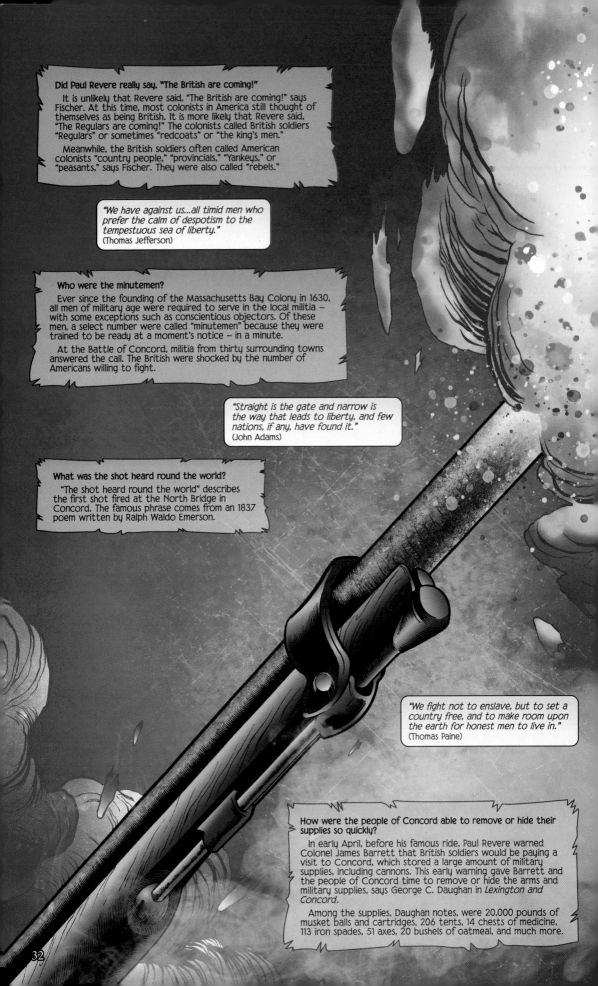

Did Paul Revere really say, "The British are coming!"

It is unlikely that Revere said, "The British are coming!" says Fischer. At this time, most colonists in America still thought of themselves as being British. It is more likely that Revere said, "The Regulars are coming!" The colonists called British soldiers "Regulars" or sometimes "redcoats" or "the king's men."

Meanwhile, the British soldiers often called American colonists "country people," "provincials," "Yankees," or "peasants," says Fischer. They were also called "rebels."

"We have against us...all timid men who prefer the calm of despotism to the tempestuous sea of liberty."
(Thomas Jefferson)

Who were the minutemen?

Ever since the founding of the Massachusetts Bay Colony in 1630, all men of military age were required to serve in the local militia – with some exceptions such as conscientious objectors. Of these men, a select number were called "minutemen" because they were trained to be ready at a moment's notice – in a minute.

At the Battle of Concord, militia from thirty surrounding towns answered the call. The British were shocked by the number of Americans willing to fight.

"Straight is the gate and narrow is the way that leads to liberty, and few nations, if any, have found it."
(John Adams)

What was the shot heard round the world?

"The shot heard round the world" describes the first shot fired at the North Bridge in Concord. The famous phrase comes from an 1837 poem written by Ralph Waldo Emerson.

"We fight not to enslave, but to set a country free, and to make room upon the earth for honest men to live in."
(Thomas Paine)

How were the people of Concord able to remove or hide their supplies so quickly?

In early April, before his famous ride, Paul Revere warned Colonel James Barrett that British soldiers would be paying a visit to Concord, which stored a large amount of military supplies, including cannons. This early warning gave Barrett and the people of Concord time to remove or hide the arms and military supplies, says George C. Daughan in *Lexington and Concord*.

Among the supplies, Daughan notes, were 20,000 pounds of musket balls and cartridges, 206 tents, 14 chests of medicine, 113 iron spades, 51 axes, 20 bushels of oatmeal, and much more.

EPIC. EDUCATIONAL. ENTERTAINING.

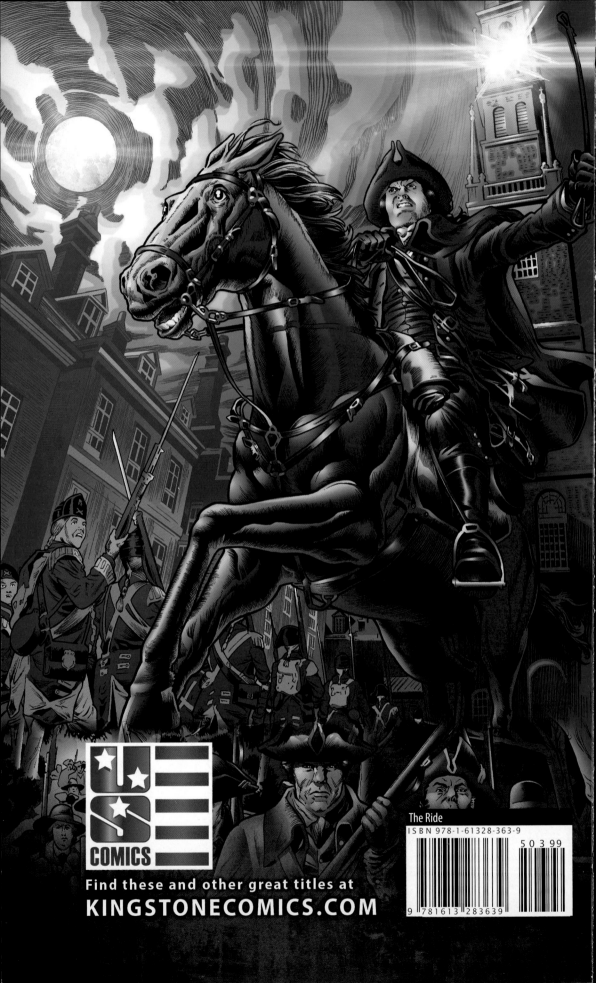

The Ride
ISBN 978-1-61328-363-9
9 781613 283639
50399